inward

inward

yung pueblo

Andrews McMeel
PUBLISHING®

two of the great lessons humanity
will learn in the 21st century will be:

to harm another is to harm oneself

when you heal yourself, you heal the world

reclaim your power,
heal yourself,
love yourself,
know yourself—
these phrases are becoming
more and more common. *why?*

because they are the pathways to
our own freedom and happiness

contents

distance

before i could release
the weight of my sadness
and pain, i first had
to honor its existence

i was never addicted
to one thing;
i was addicted to filling
a void
within myself
with things other
than my own love

to solely
attempt
to love others
without first loving yourself
is to build a home
without a strong foundation

three things make life harder:

not loving yourself
refusing to grow
not letting go

i lived so long
with a closed heart,
not because
i was afraid to get hurt
but because i was afraid
of the pain
i had hidden away

before we can
heal and let go,
what ails us
deeply
must first
come to the
surface

i spent so much time
creating versions of myself
that were far from the truth,
characters i would perform
depending on who was around

layers that could hide
the inner dance of turmoil,
between my lack of confidence,
the pain i did not understand,
and the uneasiness that comes
with reaching out to others for the
love that i was not giving myself

(before the healing)

i kept running away
from my darkness
until i understood
that in it i would
find my freedom

many of us walk the earth as strangers to ourselves,
not knowing what is true, why we feel what we feel,
actively working to repress experiences or ideas that are
too jarring for us to observe and release. it is a paradox
occurring in the human mind: we run away from what
we do not want to face, from what brings feelings of
pain, and from problems we don't have answers to,
but in our running away from ourselves we are also
running away from our own freedom.

it is through the observation of all that we are and
accepting what we observe with honesty and without
judgment that we can release the tension that creates
delusions in the mind and walls around the heart. this
is why the keys to our freedom lie in our darkness:
because when we observe our darkness by bringing our
light of awareness inward, the ego begins to dissipate
into nothingness and the subconscious slowly becomes
understood.

the mind is full of shadows, but shadows cannot
withstand the patience and perseverance of light—our
minds can become like stars, powerful united fields of
pure light. but unlike a star, the healed mind will dwell
in awareness and wisdom.

when we disconnect
from our pain
we stop growing

when we are dominated
by our pain
we stop growing

freedom is observing our pain
letting it go
and moving forward

(middle path)

it is not love
if all they want
from you
is to fulfill
their expectations

one of my greatest
mistakes
was believing
that another person
could hold together
all the pieces of me

make sure
the walls
you build
to protect yourself
do not become a prison

changes in the external world can cause great
misery when we do not know how to engage and
heal ourselves. moments of pain and discomfort, or
encounters with ideas that may break the mental
images we have created of the world, are normally
things we not only run away from but also things we
build walls to defend ourselves from. these walls we
build in our minds and hearts make sense when we
don't know any better. we all have the right to protect
ourselves from pain, but be aware that these walls
can turn from protection into prison—the more walls
we build around ourselves, the less space we have to
grow and be free. we have a harder time releasing the
habits that cause misery when we are surrounded by
the psychological walls we have constructed, causing us
to stagnate and fall into a rhythm where we are always
running within a space that is slowly growing smaller.

the opposite of this mode of being is to have a practice
that helps us go deep within ourselves to dissolve the
walls, to heal the patterns that cause us pain, to release
burdens and traumas, and to discover the universe
that dwells inside each of us. when we journey inward
and release the blocks that we first built as walls, we
naturally begin to create a new and wider space of
awareness. now when things happen in the external
world, we have more space and time to examine
how we would like to respond as opposed to reacting
blindly and reinforcing old patterns.

the body contains
our past emotions

healing work
creates space
for the release
of what we felt
long ago

don't run away
from heavy emotions

honor the anger;
give pain the space
it needs to breathe

this is how we let go

reminder:

when the body is tired
the mind will often create
worries to focus on

ask yourself often:

am i observing the situation
accurately or am i projecting how
i feel onto what is happening?

sometimes
we feel like exploding—
not because of anything
or to hurt anyone

but simply
because we are growing,
releasing,
letting the old parts die,
so that new habits,
new ways of being,
have space to live

(shedding)

sometimes deeper mental clarity
is preceded by great internal storms

healing yourself can be messy

seeing yourself through honesty
can be jarring and tough; it can even
temporarily cause imbalance in your life

it is hard work to open yourself
up to release your burdens

like removing thorns from your body,
it may hurt at first, but it is
ultimately for your highest good

the dark clouds of rainfall are
necessary for new growth

an apology to past lovers:

i wasn't ready
to treat you well

i didn't know love
was meant to be selfless

i didn't know my pain
had control over my actions

i didn't know how far away
i was from myself
and how that distance
always kept us miles apart

(blind heart)

when passion
and attachment
come together,
they are often
confused for love

i spent most
of my life
trying to prove
to myself and others
that i had no pain
and felt no sorrow

some people hit rock bottom before
they change themselves drastically
because at that distance they can
best see who they really want to be

questions:

am i being honest with myself?

am i allowing myself the space to heal?

am i being compassionate and patient toward
myself when i am not meeting my goals as
quickly as i had intended?

am i doing what i need to do to thrive?

ego is
self-doubt
self-hatred
anxiety
narcissism
fear of others
harshness
impatience
a lack of compassion
and illusions

ego sees problems

consciousness sees solutions

ego is not just the idea that we are better and more important than others; it most often arises in the form of fear-driven emotions that grip our mind when we no longer believe ourselves capable of great things, when we look down on ourselves and treat ourselves harshly.

ego makes us see the world through fearful illusions; it makes us give the same punishing treatment we give ourselves to other people.

ego is a cloud that surrounds consciousness and disturbs its clarity. when we grow our self-love, our ego diminishes; when we purify ourselves and let go of mental burdens, the ego loses its power. as we learn to heal ourselves, we do not hate our ego, nor do we become complacent with the limitations it imposes on our lives. the highest happiness, the deepest sense of freedom, an unshakeable peace is possible when the ego no longer reigns, when the love of consciousness can flow without interruption.

the world itself is currently shifting from being ruled by the fear of ego to being liberated by the love of consciousness; what we face internally is a microcosm of what humanity faces globally—this is why growing our self-love is a medicine for our earth.

if you measure
the length
of your ego,
it will equal
the distance
between you
and your freedom

if you
are far away
from yourself,
how could
you ever be
close to another?

what is happening within us
will reveal itself in the energy
of our actions and words

honesty creates intimate connections
and decreases the turbulence of life

dishonesty creates distance and problems
that have to be dealt with in the future

if we are
not growing,
then we are
probably hurting

there is not a single moment when change is not
present. the constant of the universe, the motion of
impermanence, is observably evident in the world
around us and the world within us.

if we examine nature, it is clear that everything is in
a constant state of dynamic change. trees are a great
example: in cycles they alternate from experiences of
growth to experiences of releasing, all the while alive,
all the while growing. if we are refusing to grow, then
we are moving against the flow of nature; the flow
of change is so powerful that resisting it can only
cause difficulty.

sometimes growth hurts, but it is the type of pain
that is easier to endure because it is helping us come
forward as a better version of ourselves.

the greatest gift
sadness gave me
was the motivation
to transform

do not let a cloudy mind trick you
into doing things you are done with

reminder:

you can love people and
simultaneously not allow
them to harm you

the most widespread affliction
that people suffer from is a lack
of belief in their own power

to be so broken
to have
f a l l e n
so deeply
that the only thing
you can do is
r i s e
into a new you

(phoenix)

union

the healer
you have been
looking for
is your own courage
to know and love
yourself completely

it did not
happen overnight
and it was not
given to me by another

i am the maker
of the happiness and love
growing within me

make your growth
sustainable
by moving at a pace
that is challenging
but not overwhelming

there is a tendency to doubt
your growth in the midst of a
big leap forward; hold steady
and allow yourself to bloom

i do not wish
to change the past

it made me
who i am today

i only want
to learn from it
and live in a new way

letting go
doesn't mean forgetting;
it means we stop carrying
the energy of the past
into the present

healing begins with acceptance and culminates in
letting go.

when a great misery occurs, it remains with us for as
long as we hold on to it. attachments form because
of the energy we use to keep what happened, or the
image of what we want to happen, locked away within
our mind and body—this is the cause of tension in
our being. when we hold on to these attachments,
they travel with us as a burden, from our past, to our
present, and into our future. they can even be passed
on to our descendants long after we are gone.

the miracle of healing ourselves is so powerful,
because in the movement of accepting and letting go,
we relinquish the energy of burden not only in our
present but in our past and future as well. imagine the
time line of your life. now imagine the burdens that
you carry as an extra line layered on top. as we let go
of our miseries, this extra layer becomes thinner and
thinner. it will not change what happened, but the
extra energy we carried because of these occurrences
will no longer weigh down the time line of our life.
what happened, happened, but now these moments
are no longer attachments of pain and sorrow; now
they are experiences we learn from, lessons that bring
us into a present of greater freedom, happiness,
and wisdom.

when you grow rapidly
and experience
such deep insights
that you can no longer
look at yourself
or the world
in the same way

be kind
allow yourself
the time and space
to settle into the new you

(integrate)

let's make
s p a c e
for deep healing
in our world

a real sign
of progress
is when we no longer
punish ourselves
for our imperfections

you have
walked through fire
survived floods
and triumphed
over demons
remember this
the next time you doubt
your own power

she believed that the damage
to her mind and heart was permanent,
until she met wisdom, who taught her
that no pain or wound is eternal, that all
can be healed, and that love can grow
even in the toughest parts of her being

ask yourself:

is this worry real or is my mind just
looking for something to grab onto?

the mind is a series of patterns

if we wish to change ourselves
we should create new habits

when we build new habits
we are creating a new life

we carry
our attachments
and pain
in our bodies;
as we let them go
our bodies change

a body is a field of moving energy and a system of information. as life continues its fluctuations, we tend to gather attachments, burdens, and sorrows. we hold them so tightly that they become embedded in the body, causing blockages and disruptions in the flow of our system, which can limit access to the best possible version of ourselves—this sometimes manifests as ailments or disease as well as a lack of belief in our own power and a lack of understanding of the universe.

when we use purifying healing techniques, the body begins releasing these knots of attachment, allowing our field of energy to return to balance and move more freely and powerfully. this causes changes in our body: not just physical changes, such as the healing of disease or ailments, but immaterial and internal changes as well, such as believing in oneself more, the growth of love, and the aspiration to grow into wisdom. really, there is no separation between the mind and the body; they move together as one under the leadership of our mental contents.

if you spend too long not
letting yourself be creative
you can literally start feeling sick

you were born to create
let it flow, do not overthink it

i am not fully healed
i am not fully wise
i am still on my way
what matters is that
i am moving forward

i knew i was on the right path when
i started feeling peace in situations
where i would normally feel tension

find the tools you need to heal

every time i meet more of myself
i can know and love more of you

a person
grows in beauty
whenever they
move away from
what harms them and
into their own power

never forget
the ones who
saw greatness
in you even in your
darkest moments

where do good decisions come from?
a calm mind

how can you measure your peace?
by how calm you stay during a storm

how do you know if you are attached to something?
because it creates tension in your mind

where are the greatest revolutions fought and won?
in the heart

do you know why you are powerful?
because you can change the future

feed your fire
cleanse your air
tend your earth
treat your water

(self-care)

progress
is when we
forgive ourselves
for taking so long
to treat our bodies
like a home

in one lifetime we can
be reborn many times

and so she moves forward,
with a little more wisdom,
a heart that is more open
to love, and a mind
that welcomes deep healing

(release)

i feel victorious
and free every moment
i do not measure my
personal value by
the things i do or own

a partner
who supports your dreams
and your healing
is a priceless gem,
a heaven in human form

(selfless love)

a hero
is one who heals
their own wounds
and then shows others
how to do the same

i started speaking
my truth
when being free
became more
important than guarding
the fear of my ego

her rebirth was stunning—
she lifted herself up from
the depths of despair,
grasped her dreams,
embedded them in her heart,
and walked forward into
a future that only her will
and vision could control

(revival)

i closed my eyes
to look inward
and found a universe
waiting to be explored

much of my confusion and sadness came from
being disconnected from myself. the greatest
journey i have taken so far is the one where i ended
the alienation between me and all that i am, the one
where i connected my light and my darkness, where
i united what i wanted to know with what i did not
want to face. only through this union and truthfulness
did i begin to feel at home within my own being.

(coming home)

forcing ourselves
to be happy is not
genuine or useful

being honest
about what we feel,
while remaining calm
and aware,
is the real work

reminder:

a sign of growth is being
okay with not being okay

there is an important difference between dwelling in
misery and understanding that on the path of healing
things will come up that sometimes cause us to feel
the old emotions and patterns that we are working on
letting go.

there is great power in honoring the reality of our
current emotions—not feeding them or making them
worse but simply recognizing that this is what has
arisen in this present moment and that this will
also change. when we create this space within
ourselves—a space of calmness that is undisturbed
by the storm—the storm tends to pass more quickly.

practicing such profound honesty within ourselves
helps in all facets of internal and external life—there is
no real freedom without honesty, and without honesty,
there can be no peace of mind.

healing ourselves isn't about constantly feeling bliss;
being attached to bliss is a bondage of its own. trying
to force ourselves to be happy is counterproductive,
because it suppresses the sometimes tough reality of
the moment, pushing it back within the depths of our
being, instead of allowing it to arise and release.

healing ourselves is the personal movement we embark
on to let go of all the conditioning that limits our
freedom; in this journey there will undoubtedly be
moments of bliss and difficulty. real happiness and
wisdom grow from the reality we experience, not from
the fleeting moments of bliss that we feel.

the more love
in my body,
the less harm
my body can do

who i am is always changing,
not because i am being fake
but because i am always open
to growth and transformation

it may have taken a long time,
but in the end it did not matter.
after much healing through
self-observation she now had
strength, she now had courage,
and the wisdom to wield her new
magic with virtue. no longer did
she run from her pain or her
troubles, no longer did she allow
delusions to capture her mind, no
longer did she doubt that the greatest
healer she has ever met is her own
unconditional love.

(you are a healer)

dear moon,

thank you for shedding light in the darkness,
for helping me know myself better than before, for
giving time and magic to the earth and order to our
nightly stars. you are a mother who sees all, knows all,
and asks for nothing in return.

i trust the ones
who are always
seeking to grow

the undeniable radiance of
someone who is not afraid
to grow, be free, and thrive

find someone you can heal with

i want a love that doesn't break
one that gives me water
when i am consumed by fire
one that offers me shelter
when i am lost
one that helps me see
that the hero
i am looking for
is me

(partners)

real love began when we
both stopped expecting and
instead focused on giving

many forms of modern-day love contain conditions,
meaning that we have an idea that we want those we
feel deeply for to fulfill. sometimes we don't see our
hopes and expectations for the ones closest to us as
conditional forms of love, because we perceive what
we want for them as "good." unknowingly, in our
wanting of what is "best" for them we limit our ability
to give them the finest and most powerful form of
love, a selfless love that empowers them to decide for
themselves what is best for their lives.

so much of what we think is love is actually
attachment and expectation. focusing on giving in
our relationships isn't easy; it is a habit that requires
strengthening, repetition, healing our minds, and
allowing our selfless nature to come forward for it to
become our new normal. there is a special harmony
that arises when two people focus on giving more
to each other, a subtle communication and growing
awareness between them that allows for better support
of each other's happiness.

we may worry, "how will i ensure that what i desire
is met?" a better question may be, "has solely
focusing on meeting my desires truly brought me
happiness?" the happiest people, the ones who have
successfully purified their minds of all conditioning and
craving, tend to have such a strong compassion and
understanding of love that their lives naturally focus on
giving to others. in this giving and clarity of mind they
find happiness.

though most of us are far from having fully liberated
minds, it is always worth understanding that giving is
one of the most powerful forces we can set in motion,
that through giving we not only support those around
us but also wisely follow the law of nature—everything
we do will ultimately come back to us in some form
or another. if everyone focuses on giving, we will each
receive more.

they were wrong.
this pain, this heartache,
these harmful habits,
they don't last forever

why? because the heart
is made of water and
the mind is made of fire—
the essence of both is change

the will to heal can remove
the deepest stains on our spirit

progress is being aware when there
is a storm happening inside of you
and remaining calm as it passes by

what does it mean to "live in love"?

it means to rise above judgment so that we may see the
world and ourselves with eyes of compassion. it means
allowing the wisdom of love to orchestrate our actions,
to always seek to produce thoughtful movements that
support the good of all beings, and to emit peace into
the ocean of humanity with our every step. living in
love is allowing ourselves to move through life with
an open heart so that all may share in the gift of our
goodwill and kindness. it is to ask ourselves, "how
would love heal this situation?" before we make
our move.

i want to live in a world where harm
is not systemic, where love organizes
society, where the earth is respected,
and where life is valued above all else

anyone who is willing
to know themselves,
to face themselves with
honesty and work toward
loving themselves and
all beings without condition,
is a hero who is adding to the
collective peace of humanity

two things are true:

people who truly know and love themselves
cannot be hateful toward other people

the same way we are anchored and grounded
by the earth, the earth is healed and nurtured
by our unconditional love

a human is as deep as an ocean,
yet most of us spend our lives
knowing only the surface

when we decide to dive deep
within ourselves, we set in motion
the miracle of personal evolution

(deeper healing)

though the pain
once felt unbearable
and everlasting,
the peace i feel today
is a testament to the
heart's ability to heal

all along i have searched for
knowledge when what i was
really looking for was wisdom

not the information that fills
my mind with details and facts

but the experiences that fill
my being with freedom,
healing, and the light of insight

(liberation)

then came the day
when i looked into a mirror
and saw ten thousand faces;
in that moment i understood
that my body not only holds
a multitude of stories
but that i also exist
in many places
and many times
at once

(timeless)

rebirth:

the moment people
wake up to their power
and start moving
toward their freedom

my mission
is to heal
my mind
with wisdom
and to infuse
my body
with love

allow yourself to transform
as many times as you need
to be fully happy and free

the inward movement can be summarized as follows: we observe ourselves, we accept what we find without judgment, we let it go, and the actual release causes our transformation.

we are already always changing, but when we focus on healing, we can change in the direction of our choosing; these are moments when we intentionally reclaim our power. every moment we take to know ourselves, we return as someone new.

whatever calms and concentrates the mind causes the purifying release of old burdens that weigh us down. one can be successful with simple inward observation, but when we observe ourselves through proven healing techniques, including different forms of meditation and practices of yoga asanas, among many other things, we accelerate the process of change.

different techniques reach different levels of the mind. ultimately, any practice that you feel is challenging but not overwhelming and is giving you real results is the right one for you at the moment. as we progress, we may take on sharper tools for deeper healing. anything that can heal the subconscious of our mind and create space for love is powerful enough to completely change our lives.

when things get tough, remember that we are not
building something small, we are building a palace of
peace within our own hearts. it takes determination
and effort to complete something of such beauty and
magnitude.

when you want to change yourself, do not change
everything at once. pick a few things to focus on first.
setting yourself up for success is key.

trying to change too many things at once is sometimes
overwhelming. being consistent with a few changes,
applying them in your life until they become integrated
as new positive habits, helps you build a strong
foundation for future transformations. setting yourself
up for victory helps you build momentum; it makes
the consistency required to achieve greater goals in the
future much more attainable.

goal:

find the balance
between being
productive and
being patient

letting go is medicine
that heals the heart

letting go is a habit
that requires practice

letting go is best done
through feeling, not thinking

heaviness comes from hanging on tightly to emotions
that were always meant to be ephemeral. it is not easy
to let go, especially when all we know is attachment.
we want things to last forever and we turn difficult
moments into long-lasting pain simply because we
have not learned to let go. we have not learned that
the beauty of living comes from the movement of
change. letting go does not mean that we forget, and
it does not mean that we give up. it just means that we
are not letting our present happiness be determined by
things that happened in the past or by things we wish
to happen in the future.

there is no mystery to
the miracle of self-healing;
it is courage, commitment,
and consistency that move us
from misery to inner peace

i gathered my habits
and started releasing
the ones that can
never lead me to
lasting freedom and joy

i am making more time for the
people who make me want to
be the best version of myself

as her love grew, her ability to feel the
unseen and listen to the wisdom of the
eternal strengthened. the walk on the path
to freedom had changed her; though she
still experienced times of difficult release,
the feeling of unity remained ever present
in her body. now that she lived her life in
the grassy field between mortality and the
infinite, she could feel that the space in
her heart was the same as the heart of
the earth and the heart of the universe.

(awareness)

~~thank you for making me happy~~

thank you for supporting my happiness

i am
at my
strongest
when
i am calm

it is the things
you say no to
that really show
your commitment
to your growth

when chaos is all around you
the wisest choice is to create
peace within you

your peace shines outward
and supports the creation
of a new harmony

(meditation)

we live in a unique time, when fear-driven and hateful
emotions are coming to the surface so that they can be
completely released, so that we can create a new world
where institutionalized forms of harm are no longer
factors in our lives. as it works for the individual, it
also works for the collective of humanity—we can't
heal what is ignored, nor can we live happily and freely
if we continue running away from our own darkness.

personally, my faith is in people. our courage to
turn inward in the hope of uncovering and releasing
all that stands in our way of becoming beings of
unconditional love is what will bring harmony and
peace to our world. unity with those around us is most
possible when we become internally whole and loving.
wisdom more easily flows through us when our minds
and hearts are no longer reacting to the suffering of
everyday life. this does not mean that we will become
cold or distant; it means that we will learn to respond
calmly to the inevitable changes of life without causing
ourselves misery. we will learn to respond to life as
opposed to blindly reacting to it.

humans affect one another deeply, in ways that the
world at large is just beginning to understand. when we

begin healing ourselves, it sets off waves that connect
us to those who have healed in the past and those
who will heal in the future. when we heal ourselves,
it gives strength to those who need more support to
take on their own personal healing journey. what we
do reverberates throughout time and space—like a rock
thrown into a lake, the circles it creates move in
all directions.

as she looked into her past,
she noticed that the road
she had traveled was
no simple straight line.
her journey toward fully
loving herself and the world
was full of forward and
backward movement,
twists, turns, detours,
and even some pauses.
at times, she doubted her progress,
her potential, and even
her power to change.
but today, with the
wisdom of experience at hand,
she knows she could not have gotten
to where she is without every
movement she has ever made.

(experience)

serious transformations begin
with two commitments:

the *courage* to try new
things and act in new ways

the *honesty* needed to no longer
hide from or lie to ourselves

the people
with the power
to move and act through
unconditional love
will be the healers and heroes
of our planet

(a new balance)

interlude

there was a woman who lived in a small town near a
tall mountain. she had lived in her beloved town all
her life. everyone in the community thought highly of
her and appreciated her kindness and calm manner.
she lived a quiet life and worked as any other
normal person.

those close to her knew that she was a dedicated
meditator, that she sat silently for a few hours a day
in deep self-observation. when they would ask her why
she took meditation so seriously, she would simply
respond by saying, "i like to learn and peace
is important to me."

as time went by, her calmness continued to grow and a
saintly radiance became apparent in her eyes—but only
a few were aware that a great change had happened
within her. a day came when she told those closest to
her that she would soon be leaving the town to live by
herself near the top of the mountain. when asked why
she was leaving, she merely stated, "it is time for me to
fully unlock my freedom." some tried to dissuade her,
but most trusted her and felt comfort knowing that the
mountain was close by.

a decade quickly and quietly passed. the people began
thinking of her as their guardian angel because ever
since she had moved up the mountain, the town had
become calmer and more prosperous; they imagined
that it might be from the good energy that she
regularly emitted.

there was a group of young people in the town who had vague memories of this woman who was slowly becoming a living legend. they were curious and hungry for wisdom from someone who had become a being of complete freedom. it had somehow become common knowledge that she had accomplished this goal. none of them had seen her since they were children, but they heard stories from people who would occasionally venture up the mountain to visit her. those who saw her would return to the town inspired and rejuvenated.

one day the young people gathered their courage and decided that it was time to pay her a visit. they organized their questions, packed light bags for a short trip, and made their way to the mountain in hopes of sharing in the woman's clarity.

the following are a few of the questions and answers between the young people and the one who is free.

they asked her,

"how did you free yourself?"

she answered,

"by embracing my own power."

they asked her,

"what does it mean to love yourself?"

she answered,

"it means to uncover and release whatever keeps you
from true happiness; to love, honor, and accept every
single part of you, especially those that are kept in
the dark. it means to observe yourself continually
with the utmost honesty and without judgment. loving
yourself means striving to reach new heights of self-
understanding so as to cultivate the wisdom that inner
peace requires."

they asked her,

"what is the key to saving the world?"

she answered,

"you. you are the key. heal yourself, know yourself, make yourself whole and free. release all limits so that your love can flow unconditionally for yourself and the world. this will open the heaven of your heart and it will guide you without fail."

they asked her,

"why are we here at a time when
there is so much misery and despair?"

she responded,

"because you answered the call. the earth signaled for
heroes, and the heavens sent forth the ones who were
most ready to grow and unleash their unconditional
love. you're here to shine the light of your own
healing, to offer the world the gift of your balance
and peace."

they asked her,

"are you wealthy?"

she responded,

"yes. it took years to build, but now there
is a palace in my heart that i have constructed
out of awareness, calmness, and wisdom."

they asked her,

"what is true power?"

she answered,

"true power is living the realization that you are your
own healer, hero, and leader. it is when you share your
truth with compassion and peace. your power grows
when you make progress in your own freedom and
wisdom. those who are truly powerful do not harm
themselves or others; instead, they use their energy to
enrich all they know with love."

self-love

self-love
is the beginning:
an essential centerpiece
that opens the door
to unconditional love
for yourself and all beings

self-love is a sincere
acceptance of the past

an agreement to make
the most of the present

and a willingness to allow
the best to occur in the future

(wholehearted)

self-love
is the nourishment
that gives us
the clarity and strength
to love others well

self-love is personal evolution in action

being honest
with yourself
is an act of
self-love

self-love
is creating space
in your life to heal
your body and mind

do not confuse self-love
with thinking that you're
better than everyone else

true self-love is accepting
yourself for all that you are,
especially the darkest parts

the more we love ourselves, the more easily
prosperity and miracles can flow into our lives

self-love has the power to release all blocks

through self-love we can travel the universe

self-love is doing the work
we need to do to be free

self-love begins with the acceptance of where we
are now and the history we carry, but it does not
stop there. self-love is an energy we use for our own
personal evolution; it is a meeting and balance of two
critically important ideas: loving who we currently
are and simultaneously transforming into the ideal
version of ourselves. though these ideas may seem
contradictory, they are both required for our ultimate
success. without acceptance, our transformation into a
happier and freer self would be highly difficult. why?
because it is much harder to change and let go of what
we hate.

self-love helps us delve deeply into ourselves and
release the patterns in our subconscious that impact
our behavior and emotions. true self-love is when
one understands that the inward journey is the path
to freedom, that observing and releasing our inner
burdens is what will make us feel lighter and more
aware. self-love does not grow the ego; it does the
opposite. it is our ego that carries the craving that
causes our suffering—the incessant craving that rests
at the center of the ego is the ultimate block that
stops us from achieving freedom.

since true self-love
is the gateway
to unconditional love
for all beings,
this must mean
that many people
in our world are suffering
from a lack of self-love

(the missing peace)

your
self-love
is a
medicine
for the earth

as your self-love
grows stronger,
so do the waves
of change that
you can create

the beauty
of self-love
is that it can
grow into the
unconditional love
that can end all harm

with self-love, we have the determination and
courage to move deeply inward using honesty as
our guide. this inward movement transforms our
being, dramatically enhancing our awareness of who
we are, our understanding of the universe, and our
capabilities as individuals. a beautiful result of this
process is that our new sense of compassion toward
ourselves does not end with us; it blossoms and flows
outward into the lives of others and has the capacity,
if consistently cultivated, to encompass all beings.

this growing compassion becomes the centerpiece
and active component of a love that knows no
limits. unconditional love for ourselves and others
completely respects our sovereignty as individuals
and honors our power by no longer allowing
ourselves to be harmed by anyone. this limitless love
also gives us new grace and clarity that help us see
ourselves in all other beings and better understand
where they are coming from. it gives us the strength
to treat all with kindness and support all in living
lives in which they are no longer harmed.

unconditional love can bring balance to our world.
the clarity it produces can help us better understand
the roots of harm and work to eliminate them so
that all can have the external freedom needed to
work on their own internal liberation. the greed
and reactiveness that cause harm can be replaced
with love as the primary motivator and responses of
kindness as our principal form of action. to create

this shift in our world, many will have to heal
themselves deeply by doing their inner work, releasing
burdens within themselves, and creating enough space
so that their own self-love can breathe deeply and
expand into unconditional love.

as more expand into this field of greater egolessness,
the world will shift with us and be significantly relieved
of the greed that sits at the center of the imbalance
that we currently experience. our love as a humanity
does not need to be perfectly unconditional to change
the world—every time our collective love grows, it
creates a better future.

understanding

healing yourself will ask more of you

more rest
more self-love
more letting go
more time for learning
more space for transformation
more honesty about how you feel
more time developing good habits
more courage to try new practices
more faith in yourself and the process
more time cultivating your inner peace

things to practice and integrate:

unconditional self-acceptance
not harming yourself or others
patience without complacency
giving without wanting

i cannot
make you happy,
but i can
commit to support you
in the creation
of your own happiness

to expect another to resolve all of our issues and give us the happiness we desire is to expect to see the sunrise without opening our own eyes. it is to ask a river to give us nourishment without dipping our own hands into the water. another cannot answer a riddle that was only ever meant for our own minds to solve. the universe seeks to enlighten and empower us, thus it is only rational that we are our own greatest healers.

happiness may seem elusive. try as we might, no matter our external setup, happiness will come and go. the sea of life flows between calmness and storms. either something outside of us will cause us some sort of struggle or something from within us will arise that is asking to be acknowledged and released. a human being is an accumulation of aversions and cravings, which periodically rise from the depths of our mind so that we can have the opportunity to let them go. why? because our nature is not to be full of burdens; we are meant to be light, free, open to the harmony of love and the wisdom of the universe.

though happiness will come and go, we do have the power to deepen our experience of it and extend our time partaking in its heavenly nature. to do so requires effort on our part to enhance our relationship with ourselves so that we may discover all that impedes our contentment and release it from our being.

while in the midst
of serious internal growth
respect your need to rest

love is not:

i will give this to you
if you do this for me

love is:

i will give this to you
so that you may shine

true love does not hurt; attachments do

love cannot cause pain; attachments cause pain. we create attachments in our mind when we want to hold on to something or someone, or when we expect things to be a certain way. when the attachments that we create in our minds break, we feel their rupture deeply. how deeply depends on how much we identify with the image that we have created. when things happen contrary to these images that we hold dear in our minds, we feel pain from these attachments being stretched and broken.

attachments are not a form of true love. unconditional love, selfless love, a love without expectations is a higher form of existence that creates no attachments or images. it is a state of profound egolessness. expectations and judgments are attachments that the untrained mind repeatedly creates, causing more knots and burdens that impede our happiness. the typical human mind is eclipsed by the delusion of ego; the ego separates, categorizes, and labels everything that it comes across, causing our discontent and misunderstanding.

all mental tension comes from not letting go

stress and anxiety are the children of
attachment; they are both forms of craving
that take us away from the present and into
areas of imagination that steal away our peace.

wanting always interrupts being

peace makes you strong
hate reveals your emptiness
kindness feeds your happiness
anger reveals your fear
love makes you free

how to lead yourself:

1. develop a relationship with your intuition

2. have the courage to follow its guidance

i can only
give to you
what i have already
given to myself

i can only
understand
the world as much as
i understand myself

as she was swimming in the ocean of wisdom
that dwells in her heart, she understood deeply
that all was a part of her, that no one was
separate from her. she whispered lightly with
newfound peace, "i am everything." that was
when she realized that her greatest power is,
and always was, her ability to love herself.

wholeness
is when lies
no longer stand
between you
and yourself

how to improve your life:

1. make self-love a top priority

2. learn a self-healing technique

3. create space for daily healing

4. know that everything changes

5. be kind, loving, and honest to all

i am not
here to
compete

i am here
to grow
and be free

every time we compete with others, we are already
losing, because we are forgetting that life is not a
race to be won but a journey we embark on to build
our inner peace and wisdom. we create nonexistent
competitions in our minds when we get carried away
by the delusions of ego. the hierarchical conditioning
of society combined with our attachment to "i," "me,"
and "my" creates a scenario in which only a few
can succeed.

having a world built on competition has created
a situation in which humanity is overflowing with
misery—we thought we had to win, to harm each other
to survive, but the moment we submitted ourselves to
this scenario, we took a step away from our individual
and collective freedom.

releasing these conditioned habits is difficult but
essential, because happiness and internal security
grow as we release the "i" of ego and the delusion
of competition. the wisdom of love shows us that
individual and collective life need to be reborn and
reorganized in a way that supports the well-being of
all, not the few. love teaches us that we are here not
to compete but to support each other's growth
and happiness.

unconditional love sees no one as an enemy

my faith
for a better future
is in the people
who are turning the idea
of unconditional love
into a way of life

if you want to know
how free you are,
ask yourself,
"how far does
my love extend?"

there is a path
we can walk
where we no longer
allow anyone to harm us
while also loving
all beings unconditionally

fear seeks control
revenge prolongs pain
animosity disrupts peace
compassion ignites healing
honesty releases burdens
happiness is letting go

loneliness
will not
go away
if we remain
far away
from ourselves

repeat daily:

notice the stories you hold in your mind

let go of the ones that cause tension

sometimes people are simply meant to
teach you how not to act in the future

everyone is a teacher, but that does not mean everyone is correct.

there have been times in our lives when we have been a good example for those around us, while at other times we have not been a good example. if we recognize our own imperfections, it helps us have compassion for all people and look upon all as equals.

just because someone was wrong once, it doesn't mean they are going to be wrong forever. similarly, just because we may perceive someone as wrong, it does not necessarily mean that we are right. in most cases we lack the perfect information required to form an objective and universal perspective.

it is important to remember that we are all imperfect and that we all live through the limited perspective of ego.

striving to learn as much as we can from one another without making harsh and permanent judgments is a sign of wisdom.

part of
being human
is having
opportunities
to give and
receive forgiveness

i am not sure when i will
be completely free and healed,
but i do know i will feel it
more clearly than anything else
i have ever felt in my life

she's an explorer,
unafraid to travel
within her heart and mind,
ready to discover new spaces
to heal—releasing burdens
and planting wisdom wherever
her awareness takes her

the strongest
people
i have met
are the ones
who do not
harm themselves

the idea that
when you let go
of what you want,
it comes to you

working toward our goal and simultaneously letting it
go may seem paradoxical, but it is the fastest way to
achieve what we want. letting go is not giving up; it
is the graceful walk between continuing to put effort
into making our preferred reality come true and not
allowing our happiness to be controlled by something
we do not have. if we remain attached, we tend to feel
agitation or even misery. this creates tension in our
being that blocks us from fulfilling our desires.

sometimes we may still get what we want, even if we
do not know how to let go; but in these cases, we may
be less capable of keeping what we want, and it may
even cause us more misery because we never addressed
the root of our tension, which is our inability to
appreciate what we already had to begin with.

what do we get when we let go of the past and the
future? inner peace. realizing peace within ourselves
no matter our external circumstance is a high form
of freedom that allows blessings, miracles, and success
to flow into our lives. happiness and gratitude are
attractive forces; their lack of wanting is what clears the
road so that new things may come with greater ease.

water teaches flexibility and power
earth expresses firmness and balance
air sings of intelligence and bravery
fire speaks of action and growth

the mind
is a garden;
what we decide
to grow there will
determine our prosperity

bad vibes
can't hurt you
when your balance
and love are strong

sometimes
we go back and repeat
an old mistake
just so we can remember
why we moved forward

giving yourself
the space and time
to respond
instead of reacting blindly
is an important way
to reclaim your power

the body knows what it requires;
listen to it—not the cravings of
the mind but the needs of the body—
let it guide you into well-being

(intuitive healing)

your friends
who have the courage
to expand their
wisdom and self-awareness—
they are special;
keep them close

the forces
of the universe
support those
who work at
healing themselves

peaceful minds
have the power
to create
a peaceful world

when the mind feels wild and cloudy,
it may be that something from deep within
has come to the surface, an old burden
seeking release. *breathe, relax, and let it go.*

(storms)

sanity is the unwillingness to do harm

i held my fear by the hand,
honored its existence, and
thanked it for teaching me
that happiness exists beyond
the boundaries it creates

free
people
have no
masters
but themselves

movements change the world, but just as it is
important to be a part of and build movements to
create a world where human rights are a reality
for all—a world where systemic forms of social
and economic oppression no longer exist—so it is
equally important to build our own intimate internal
movement that focuses on healing the greed, hatred,
and fear within ourselves that cause so much chaos
in our lives and are the actual underlying roots of the
societal chaos we experience.

every society is simply a composition of its individuals
believing, consenting to, and perpetuating particular
stories that come together to create the world we
know. if the stories we choose to believe in change, if
we begin to understand that when we harm another we
are actually harming ourselves—not in a fictional sense
but in a literal sense, similar to the way that water is
good for the body and poison is bad—then we will
quickly shift into a new world.

pleasure cannot fill the heart
hate cannot keep you safe
anger cannot set you free
only love can fill voids
only love can create peace
only love can liberate

love
is the most
potent and versatile
form of magic

love
is the strongest
building material
in the universe

not just
the love
between people
but the love
that gives you
the power
to heal yourself
and change the world

they both know that they are not together
to complete each other, that their happiness is
their own to create. nevertheless, their ethereal bond
serves a great purpose; it gives them the time and space
to love each other well enough to release the tension of
their unloved hearts. their love for one another is not
the end but rather a means to an end. it is a humble
tool of healing and nourishment that can strengthen
their minds and make their spirits mighty, so that they
may both travel as far within themselves as possible,
so that they may both release all that limits the flow of
their happiness, so that they may both swim freely in
the waters of wisdom and universal understanding.

(love is a key)

"'strength'? what do you mean by 'strength'?"

"what i mean is how firm is your inner peace,
how honestly can you observe yourself without
judgment, how limitless is your love for yourself
and all beings, and how willing are you to change
yourself for the better?"

courage
+
letting go
+
self-love
=
a growing awareness

as our ability to
know and heal ourselves
deepens, we will be better
equipped to examine the
world more carefully
and heal it more
effectively

healing yourself with love
is a long-term process

healing the world with love
is a long-term process

i rebel by loving more

whenever we are asked to limit our love, to be selective
with our love, to reserve our love for some parts of
ourselves and not others or to reserve our love for
some people and not others, we do a disservice to
ourselves by following along, because any love withheld
becomes tension in our being.

the normality of perpetual war, the rising tide of
poverty, the varying forms of violence our economy
requires to stay afloat, and the indifference that we
are expected to feel toward it all are stifling and ever
present. when we think of happiness, it is important
to remember that, generally speaking, we fall together
and we rise together. those of us alive today have never
lived in a world where a large portion of humanity was
not struggling to meet its material needs or fighting for
the right to be treated as human beings—we humans
have the uncanny ability, whether we are aware of it or
not, to feel and be affected by the plight and struggle
of others. energy sees no barriers.

whenever we are asked to keep our eyes and hearts
closed, and we do just that, because it is easier
than accepting the responsibility of a world and
humanity that need healing, because it is easier than
understanding that to heal the world will require a
heroic effort on our part to heal our own inner world,
we are dimming the light of our own future. it is in
the challenge of allowing our love to flow actively and
limitlessly that we come to find greater degrees

of our own personal liberation and global liberation for all beings.

the dalai lama once stated, "compassion is the radicalism of our time." this is true. today we rebel by loving more. when we can see and treat each other as family, we will know a global peace.

do not forget
to send your love
into the earth
into the water
into the sky

how will you help heal the world?

by healing myself and supporting
the healing of those around me.
by allowing love to fill my very
being and guide my every action.
by understanding that if it causes
harm, it must not be the right way.

observe.

accept.

release.

transform.

because being calm in the midst
of chaos is a sign of true power

measure
your success
by the growth
of your freedom

the mind is a lot more vast than conscious thought
can comprehend. the conscious part of the mind—the
part where we feel and hear the movements of our
emotions, memories, and thoughts—may seem large,
but it is quite small in comparison to the subconscious.
an iceberg's small peak floats above water while the
great majority of its mass sits silently and unseen
underneath—the top is visible and prominent, but what
is unseen is much bigger and has a massive effect on
the part that is seen, largely dictating its movements.
the mind works in a similar manner; the subconscious
and the reactive patterns that have accumulated there
over time, though they remain mostly unknown or
forgotten, have a strong effect on our daily behavior.

this is why there is a lot more to freedom than simply
having unrestricted mobility or having our material
needs met or the removal of all forms of external
oppression. freedom is deeper than believing that
we are free on the conscious level of the mind—
the conscious may think this to be so, but if the
subconscious is still burdened with patterns that cause
us misery, delusion, and the pain that comes with
unceasing reactions, then we are not yet wholly free.
the greatest oppressor is the untrained mind.

freedom grows when we begin the mental healing and
training that teaches us how to let go and interact with
the ocean of life in a way that no longer causes us
misery; our freedom grows as we observe deep within

ourselves and begin letting go of our attachments and
burdens that clog up the subconscious mind. freedom
is happening every moment when we are not craving
something more.

the mind is purified as we release the weight of the
past and the yearnings for specific things in the
future—especially if our happiness is dependent on
obtaining these things. the mind is clear, powerful,
and effectively decisive when we can truly observe
the present moment without projecting our ego onto
it. freedom is something we build within. freedom
is a habit.

~~find yourself~~
free yourself

goals:

develop my calmness
cultivate my wisdom
expand my freedom
help heal the world

releasing,
learning,
expanding—
i am happily a
work in progress

sending love to all beings
may all beings continue reclaiming their power
may all beings heal themselves and the world
may all beings be happy and free

about the author

diego perez is the writer behind the pen name yung
pueblo. the name yung pueblo means "young people."
it serves to remind him of his ecuadorian roots, his
experiences in activism, and that the collective of
humanity is in the midst of important growth. his
favorite word, "liberation," took on a deeper meaning
once he started meditating vipassana, as taught by
s.n. goenka. through writing and speaking, he aims to
support the healing of the individual, realizing that
when we release our personal burdens, we contribute
to a global peace.

Andrews McMeel Publishing
a division of Andrews McMeel Universal
1130 Walnut Street, Kansas City, Missouri 64106

www.andrewsmcmeel.com

22 23 24 25 26 RR4 18 17 16 15 14

ISBN: 978-1-4494-9575-6

Library of Congress Control Number: 2018942082

Editor: Melissa Rhodes
Art Director/Designer: Jenny Mohrfeld
Production Editors: Elizabeth A. Garcia and Margaret Utz
Production Manager: Cliff Koehler

ATTENTION: SCHOOLS AND BUSINESSES
Andrews McMeel books are available at quantity discounts
with bulk purchase for educational, business, or sales
promotional use. For information, please e-mail the
Andrews McMeel Publishing Special Sales Department:
specialsales@amuniversal.com.

Also by *New York Times* bestselling author
yung pueblo

let go of the past
connect with the present
expand the future

lighter

yung pueblo

New York Times bestselling author
of *Clarity & Connection*

A radical plan for turning inward, becoming more self-compassionate, and lifting the heaviness that prevents us from healing ourselves and the world.

HARMONY
BOOKS · NEW YORK

Available wherever books are sold